HANDBOOKS OF EUROPEAN NATIONAL DANCES

EDITED BY
VIOLET ALFORD

DANCES OF SPAIN

I : South, Centre and North-West

Plate 1
Seguidillas Sevillanas

DANCES of SPAIN

I : South, Centre and North-West

LUCILE ARMSTRONG

NOVERRE PRESS

**ILLUSTRATED BY
LUCILE ARMSTRONG
ASSISTANT EDITOR
YVONNE MOYSE**

First published in 1953
This edition published in 2021 by
The Noverre Press
Southwold House
Isington Road
Binsted
Hampshire
GU34 4PH

ISBN 978-1-914311-13-0

© 2021 The Noverre Press

CONTENTS

	Page
INTRODUCTION	7
Andalusian Dances Classified	8
Some Andalusian Folk Dances	9
The Central Uplands	10
The North-Western Regions	11
Music	13
Costume	14
When Dancing May Be Seen	17
THE DANCES	18
Poise of Body • Arm Gestures • Basic Steps	19
Pericote	19
Danza Prima	22
Muiñeira	24
Playing of Castanets	31
Movements and Steps in Seguidillas Sevillanas	31
Seguidillas Sevillanas	36
BIBLIOGRAPHY	40

Illustrations in Colour, pages 2, 12, 29, 39
Map of Spain, page 6

INTRODUCTION

To most non-Spaniards 'Spanish' dancing means Andalusia. As we shall see, this is an entirely false idea, but to please the great majority we will begin with that vast southern province.

The southern part of the Peninsula was dominated by the Moors for seven hundred years, their culture spreading throughout the land. Arts, learning, sciences, traditions, blood, show strong Moorish influence. Dancing is no exception. The famous back-bends, the play of delicate hands and fingers are Eastern rather than European, but certain aspects are older than the Moors. So intensely developed, so severely stylised a dance form is unknown save in the Orient. A definite similarity between Indian and Andalusian style can be noted—movements of arm, hand and eyes, hand-clapping and heels rapping out broken rhythm are all non-European.

Nevertheless woman predominates, attracts, and displays her flashing graces. The man accompanies her, acts as a frame for her poses. Here lives a tradition of solo dances, and in these the man comes into his own, sinuous as an eel in his tight trousers, rapping out his *taconeado* with amazing virility; the next instant, as though by an electric shock, petrified into an arrogant statue. His expression is one of intense concentration; he seems to mesmerise his partner. The face reflects every kind of expression. No European school of dance has been so persistently studied as the school of Andalusia, every aspect of body and costume dissected and stylised to get the most striking results.

ANDALUSIAN DANCES CLASSIFIED

The several hundreds of Andalusian dances fall into three categories: (1) Flamenco; (2) Clasico Español; (3) folk dances.

The foundations of Flamenco are in the soil, probably in the soil of Cadiz, whence went the famous Gaditanae to inflame the banqueters of Rome, as told by the younger Pliny, Strabo and others. This is the most flashy type, chiefly seen in taverns and café-cabarets. It is folk dance, but folk dance assimilated by Gypsies and now performed chiefly by them though not originated by them. Flamenco dancers are inspired into improvisation by their audience and never do a dance twice in the same way. Hence the innumerable variants. So long as they remain within the framework of a dance every licence for improvisation is given. *Flamenco* literally is *Flemish*, or a braggart returned from the Flemish wars, but there are controversies about its original meaning as applied to music and dance.

Clasico Español is learnt in the dancing schools and seen on the stage. Teachers compose their dances upon a foundation of both Flamenco and folk dance, but a folk dance thus stylised becomes almost unrecognisable. To acquire mastery of these two types needs long years of training, girls beginning when tiny children. This is the only style seen outside Spain except for an exported Cuadro Flamenco.

Folk dances as performed by the country people differ from one district to another. They are just as strenuous as the first two types but a good deal easier, as they are for recreation not for exhibition. These are the dances enjoyed at any family or village fiesta, when relations and friends used to arrive—local costumes unfortunately are dying out even in Spain—in gay, frilled skirts and bright Manila shawls, the men in light grey or sleek black, with a bright kerchief round the neck. They gather round the guitarist and the *jaleo* begins. Numberless small glasses of sherry (*xerez*) soon take effect. The guitarist thrums his chords, waiting; hands begin their amazing claps; suddenly a dancer springs up inspired, claps sharply four times to proclaim the fact that he (or she) holds the floor, and on the fifth beat off he goes, the guitarist following—by no means leading. Excitement grows, ' olé, olé! ' rings out, the pace quickens, to end in a sudden frozen pose. Shouts of approval reward the dancer, who retires as four more claps are heard and another springs out. The night has just begun.

SOME ANDALUSIAN FOLK DANCES

These are some of the favourite folk dances seen on such an occasion, summarised to simplify their complexity:

ALEGRÍAS. 3/4 or 6/8. Twenty or thirty variants, with or without castanets. A woman's solo dance. In Cadiz and Granada the dress is sometimes a long, trained skirt with many frills. *Taconeado* (heel-tapping) and deft swirls of the train by the foot are constant features.

BOLERO. 3/4. Almost as many variants as the Alegrías. With castanets. A solo or dance for one couple. The Bolero was stylised during the 17th and 18th centuries. It belongs to both the stage and folk categories.

BULERÍAS. 3/4 or 6/8. A solo with finger-clicks and hand twists.

FANDANGO. 3/4 or 6/8. Very quick footwork required and very exhausting. With or without castanets. From the Fandango the Jota is said to be derived.

FANDANGUILLO. A derivative of the Fandango, with castanets and much footwork. Modern.

FARRUCA. A solo for man or woman with finger clicks. A modern stylisation of bullfighters' attitudes.

FOLÍAS. A widely-spread, very elastic, true folk dance.

OLÉ. Gaditanian (Cadiz) folk dance of apparently great antiquity. A solo with castanets.

PANADEROS. 3/4, with castanets. A folk dance for two or four people.

POLOS. For one couple. A favourite in the 18th century.

SEGUIDILLAS. A name given to a series of couplets separated by an Estribillo or Chorus. Each couplet has three parts. There are Seguidillas Sevillanas, Seguidillas Malagueñas, Rondeñas, even Manchegas, Andalusian influence having spread into La Mancha. Steps, rhythm and music vary according to the region. For one couple or groups of couples, with castanets.

SOLEARES. A dress with a train is traditional.

TANGO. This Andalusian folk and stage dance has no connection with the Argentine Couple dance. It is said to be much older. Quick 2/4 rhythm, from which extraordinary heel and toe work extracts marvels. Believed to originate in Córdova. The hat plays an important part.

VITO. 6/8. A solo danced on a table. Heel and toe work in broken rhythms.

ZAMBRA and ZORONGO. Solo dances, sinuous and of obvious Moorish origin. Cymbals or tambourine may be used with finger clicks.

THE CENTRAL UPLANDS

Castile, Extremadura, León. Leaving the hot sunshine of Andalusia, we cross the Sierra Morena and go north.

Peasants in the Salamanca region are Charros and their dances are Charradas. Leaping men but almost static women show the North is at hand. A table separates the couple in a Charrada, the man performing showy steps at each corner, the woman, one arm raised, almost shuffling round the table. When a great cake is placed thereon, the dance becomes La Rosca. At weddings an Apple dance demands coins stuck in the fruit as part of the dowry, and in return the bride dances with every man in the company.

Avila, the arid home of the great Saint Teresa, favours two concentric circles of women, unmarried ones in the middle. The men form a third circle on the outside, and claim two partners before whom they show off their steps.

Castile and León know Giraldillas, Jotas, Fandangos, even Seguidillas—an influence from the South. The geographical position of the Central regions makes them a melting-pot for surrounding provinces, which may explain the vast number of dances found here.

THE NORTH-WESTERN REGIONS

Cantabria, Asturias, Galicia. Here the type of dancing is much simpler than in the South and the style is easy for Northern Europeans to acquire. Hundreds of regional dances exist, of which the merest outline is here given. Fandangos—the Andalusian name reappearing—and Jotas are perhaps the most widely spread; ring dances of all types, the single file called the Snake, and squares for four, all are common to the Western half of Spain.

Cantabria has a lovely style shown by the Picayos—dancers who accompany Church processions—who, bowing and bending before their partners, take on the aspect of courting birds. Social dance steps are *a lo alto*, jumping high, or *a lo llano*, very smoothly, according to the dance. The girls are expert tambourine players, hardly deigning to as much as glance at the masculine display before them.

Asturias shows its own dance-expression in Danza Prima. Primitive it really seems to be, a circle moving forever clockwise, using forever the same primitive step to the monotonous strains of the same primitive tune. Danced at night by a circle of dark-clad, barely-moving people, this antique dance is deeply impressive. The Corri-Corri (running dance), a continuous seeking by the man and escaping of the woman, brings us to Galicia and the far western corner of Spain.

Plate 2
Asturias: Pericote

Shrilly plaintive bagpipes here sound across the wild valleys, calling young and old to join the Muiñeiras and the Gallegadas—the favourite Galician dances. Peasants in their brilliant regional costumes flock up the mountainsides to join the all-day-and-night fiesta. Compostella with its centuries of pilgrimages has exercised a mystic influence, bringing thousands of pious folk from other parts of Spain and from all Western Europe: facts which must be borne in mind when studying the folk arts of Galicia.

MUSIC

Andalusia. A characteristic of Andalusian dance music is very definite rhythm, as in Alegrías, Seguidillas and Pasodobles. Yet many tunes cannot be given a time-signature but must be written as musical phrases. No fast rules can be made; as in everything Andalusian it is tradition which commands. A bar of 3/4 may be followed by two bars of 3/8 or one of 5/8. No easy eight-bar music can be expected. The usual accompanying instrument for song and dance is the guitar, and in Andalusia an amazingly highly developed technique has grown up. One guitar often suffices, but guitar ensembles are used for big occasions. Guitarists, who memorise all their music (and do so by ear), are the storehouses of an immense traditional treasure.

The *bandurria* is another guitar-type instrument, generally with metal strings, and in an ensemble is used for the melody. In the dance castanets have a vital part, and in Andalusia play most intricate rhythms, though used more simply all over Spain. Finger clicks, taking the place of castanets in some dances, sound like pistol shots; so precise, so sharp are they. Finger cymbals are used in certain solo dances, tiny in size and worn on finger and thumb—an antique inheritance.

Tambourines can be used in Flamenco solo dances,

when they are large and plain. Smaller tambourines are common all over Spain.

The North-West. Bagpipes (*gaitas*) are a feature of these districts. Folk singers have an amusing habit of imitating the bagpipe, assuming a nasal tone and letting out the breath at the end of each verse with ' a dying fall ' like the wind out of the bag. The southern guitar has come to Galicia, where the player often sits on his donkey thrumming his instrument. Tambourines here are played mostly by women, and in remote mountain places amongst the Vaqueros of Alzada in Asturias, doorkeys tapped on frying-pans make percussion instruments.

Pan-pipes are common, especially for knife-grinders. Their ghostly quality seems intensified by their curious shapes such as horses' heads and Gothic windows.

The Central Provinces combine the instruments of North and South as they do the styles of dancing. Square drums are found in León.

To all these instruments the human voice must be added, for much dancing is accompanied by ' mouth music '.

COSTUME

All over Spain regional costumes are so varied and rich that a few only will be selected for description.

The South. Seville is the land of frilly cotton dresses, but satins in gay colours are paraded at the Easter fair. Seville and Malaga are the homes of the misnamed ' Spanish ' costume: high combs and lace mantillas, black for church-going, white for ' the bulls '. The usual men's costume consists of black or grey trousers cut very high above the waist and very tight round the ankle, a short jacket to match, or in summer a white one. This cut sets off to advantage the slim, arrogant figure of a dancing Andaluz. His stiff black felt hat has a broad brim, broader still at Córdova.

In Plate 3 the man wears the dark-green cloth suit of a mountain man; his peaked hat has a rolled-up brim. The woman's silk dress is decorated with pompons to match her mantilla, which is lying on the ground.

Plate 1 shows a Seville couple in fiesta costume: a silk or cotton flounced dress, brightly contrasting shoulder shawl in silk with fringe for the woman; tight black trousers, short velvet jacket with tassels and appliqué designs for the man. The trousers are cut so high that no waist sash is needed.

The North-West: Cantabria and Asturias. In both these provinces women wear chiefly red cloth skirts and black cloth bodices laced up in front, a white, wide-sleeved chemise or blouse frilled at the neck, a kerchief over the shoulders, another on the head knotted high on the crown. Men wear short trousers slit up the leg, with a red band and white frills, or long trousers and jackets to match. In parts of Asturias a velvet patch strengthens seat, elbows and collar. The costumes in Plate 2 are fiesta dresses from the Llanes district with beautiful aprons, and, for the man, a white-backed waistcoat with a design.

Galicia. Women wear red cloth skirts and black bands as in Plate 4, though vertical stripes in bright homespun are seen here and there. The shawls seem like capes crossed over the breast to tie at the back. The kerchief varies much in colour, size, and the way of knotting it. In some districts yellow skirts are preferred, but everywhere they are exceedingly wide. In the North aprons play a prominent part. Some women wear double aprons of braided cloth, a skirt, and underneath again numerous cloth petticoats of many colours.

The Galician man in this picture wears black velvet breeches with lace edging showing white pants over his knees; velvet waistcoat, woollen sash and peaked hat, the *montera*, of felt or velvet with red tassels.

Central Region. The costume of Lagartera is remarkable

even amongst the costumes of Spain. These women wear eight woollen petticoats, very short and full, each of a different colour. Wonderful embroideries make a brilliant show against the men's black apparel. Along the river valleys the most elaborate costumes are worn, whereas in the mountains the need for warmth often dictates long, full skirts of duller hues, a long apron, a crossed shawl and a kerchief over the head. Where the climate is drier, as in Cuenca and La Mancha, coloured embroideries are again seen, flowered cottons and finely worked chemises, the men flaunting elaborately embroidered knee breeches and short jacket. A kerchief round a man's head under the hat is common. These lovely costumes are rarely to be seen in towns today.

The Hair. Hairdressing is an important part of the women's costume everywhere. In Candelaria for instance the knot of hair is made to stand straight up, giving a peculiar silhouette to the figure in its mantilla. Valencia and Murcia favour 'ear-phones' kept in place by silver pins—a long tradition believed to date from Iberian times.

In the South a flat plait goes from the top of the head to the nape of the neck, and hairdressing has to accommodate high comb, mantilla, or a carnation or a rose standing straight up from the crown of the head of an Andalusian woman.

NOTE

To everybody but a Spaniard Spain means Andalusia. The text and illustrations of this Handbook show that this is not so. Do not then persist in the error. Do not dress dancers in Andalusian costumes for dances of other regions. You would be equally justified in dressing an Oxfordshire Morris man in tartan trews.

The Editor

OCCASIONS WHEN DANCING MAY BE SEEN

Carnival	Throughout the entire country, especially the Sunday, Monday and Tuesday before Lent. On these three days the Seises (choir boys) dance in Seville Cathedral.
February 2nd	Seises dance in Seville Cathedral.
Easter Tuesday	Picayos dance at San Vicente de la Barquera (Montañas de Santander). Egg Festival at Pola de Siera (Oviedo).
Week after Easter	Fair at Seville; dancing in tents. Costumes worn.
May 3rd	Festivities throughout the South and in Madrid.
Corpus Christi (Thursday after Trinity Sunday)	Great ecclesiastical processions everywhere, embracing traditional characters. Seises dance in Seville Cathedral.
Whitsunday	Seville and Huelva: Romería (pilgrimage) del Rocio in decorated carts; dances.
Ascension Day	Festivities everywhere.
June 23rd, St. John's Eve	One of the great occasions. Bonfires, dancing.
June 24th to 29th	Everywhere dancing and festivities.
August 12th	Picayos dance before the Virgen del Campo at Cabezón de la Sal (Montañas de Santander).
August 15th, Feast of the Assumption	Festivities everywhere. Pilgrimages to mountain shrines throughout the South.
August 16th	Festival at Llanes, Asturias.
September 8th	Llanes; Danza del Romance at Comillas and Ruilóba (Montañas de Santander).

A Church calendar is needed in Spain. Every Saint's Day is celebrated somewhere, every village has its Patron Saint with fiesta on that day.

[Spain, like many other countries, has emerged from the war period with her ancient practices in a state of flux. Groups with social-political leaders seem to have annexed the dances of the countryfolk, who see their inheritance interpreted by others. It is difficult now to find true traditional dancers, and the utmost caution is necessary from the traditionist's point of view as regards competitions and displays of dancing.—*The Editor.*]

THE DANCES

TECHNICAL EDITORS
MURIEL WEBSTER AND KATHLEEN P. TUCK

ABBREVIATIONS
USED IN DESCRIPTION OF STEPS AND DANCES

r—right ⎫ referring to R—right ⎫ describing turns or
l—left ⎭ hand, foot, etc. L—left ⎭ ground pattern
C—clockwise C-C—counter-clockwise

For descriptions of foot positions and explanations of any ballet terms the following books are suggested for reference:

A Primer of Classical Ballet (Cecchetti method). Cyril Beaumont.

First Steps (R.A.D.). Ruth French and Felix Demery.

The Ballet Lover's Pocket Book. Kay Ambrose.

Reference books for description of figures:

The Scottish Country Dance Society's Publications. Many volumes, from Thornhill, Cairnmuir Road, Edinburgh 12.

The English Folk Dance and Song Society's Publications. Cecil Sharp House, 2 Regent's Park Road, London, N.W.1.

The Country Dance Book I–VI. Cecil J. Sharp. Novello & Co., London.

POISE OF BODY · ARM GESTURES · BASIC STEPS

These vary considerably in the four dances included in this volume, so no general description is attempted. Under the heading 'Character' in Pericote, Danza Prima and Muiñeira some general points are given, and in these three dances the steps are described in detail. Two of these dances of the North-West are simple and one of medium difficulty.

The Andalusian example, Seguidillas Sevillanas, is in a different category and needs special study. As the Andalusian steps and gestures are very subtle, the notations for this dance are preceded on page 31 by a detailed description of body and arm movements and of the steps used.

PERICOTE (Little Peter)

Region Llanes district of Asturias.

Character A gay courting dance of great antiquity. The movement of the woman is rather quiet, the man showing great agility and variety of step. (The man's part is supposed to have been danced by a woman wearing a magic top-hat and many long coloured ribbons.) The arms are held as shown on Plate 2, and the fingers clicked in time with the music.

Formation   A trio for one man and two women. The man
—Pericote—dances his figure of eight at right
angles to the women's movement, so that the
whole ground-pattern is that of a love-knot (see
diagram).

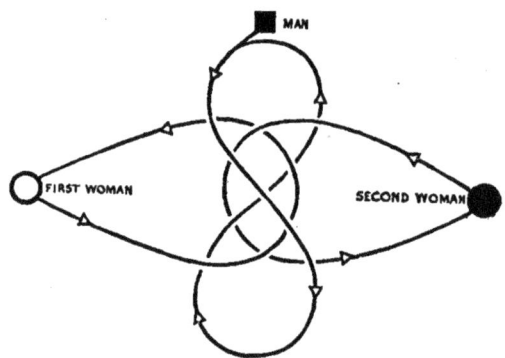

Dance   The dance allows for great variety of step for
the man, and the number of steps for each loop
may be varied, although one whole pattern
for eight bars of music is suggested.

All begin on r foot and move to R to start the figure.

The women advance towards one another, moving slightly to R, pass l shoulders with each other and retire to places passing r shoulders (back to back). The step used throughout is a shuffling walk—two steps to each bar.

The man describes a figure-of-eight pattern, passing between the women. He may use any step he likes—Pas de Basque, skip, high kick, or improvise as he goes with straight or turning movements. He shows off his own agility to the women and may draw the attention of one woman and then the other as he passes between them.

Repeat figure and music as often as desired.

PERICOTE

Llanes, Asturias. Noted by E. M. Torner
Arranged by Arnold Foster

(*This dance is played by the bagpipe and drum.*)

DANZA PRIMA

Region   Asturias, North-West region.

Character   Solemn and dignified. The ring was danced round the chapel of a hermitage, the dancers singing with no instrumental accompaniment. It is now danced in the streets, with modern words for the song.

Formation   A ring for any number of couples—men and women alternately. The dancers hold little fingers only and may enter or leave the ring at will.

Dance   The ring moves slowly C-C, the arms swinging forward and backward with a jerky movement.

The following step is used throughout:

    Step forward on r foot toward centre of circle.
    Step backward on l foot.
    Step backward on r foot (after a few repeats a slight hop on r develops).
    Step forward on l foot.

The movement is repeated continuously, the l foot remaining almost on the spot; nevertheless the ring slowly travels C-C. The steps go on regardless of change of time signatures—one step to each beat—whether the music is in 3/4 or 4/4 tempo.

DANZA PRIMA

From Asturias. Noted by E. M. Torner
Arranged by Arnold Foster

MUIÑEIRA (*The Miller's Wife*)

Region	Galicia.
Character	A gay mountain dance with castanets. Body is held with slight backward lean from the waist, the arms above the head (except during Introduction and Chorus) to represent bulls' horns. The feet are raised as high as the knee in every skipping step.
Formation	Either a couple dance—partners facing one another—or a set dance for three couples, as in diagram (O = woman, □ = man):

```
        O   3   □
        O   2   □
        O   1   □
```

Dance

	MUSIC Bars
INTRODUCTION Dancers stand still with hands on hips, facing partners.	Introduction
FIGURE I All start with r foot. Men sound the castanets on 1st and 4th beats of each bar.	A
a 4 skips forward (2 skips to each bar), advancing to partner and nodding to her on third skip. On fourth skip the l foot is placed behind the r foot.	1–2
4 skips backward, placing the l foot in front of the r foot on fourth skip.	3–4

4 skips forward as before.	5–6
3 skips turning on the spot to R about, feet together on fourth beat. (Castanets sound first beat only of bar 8.)	7–8
b All repeat movements of *a*, men skipping backward and women forward and then reversing the movement. On last four skips all turn outwards away from partner and finish facing forward with feet together.	9–16

CHORUS   B

All begin with r foot.

Couple dance. Each woman describes a wide circle C-C, the man following her with 7 gliding skip-change-of-steps. The arms swing alternately in front of and behind the body in open line (r foot forward, r arm in front, l arm behind back).	17–23
On eighth step both dancers turn sharply to R about, closing feet and raising arms above head with strong click of castanets on the first beat. Hold the arms steady with no further sound.	24
The movement is then repeated C, the man leading.	25–32
Set dance. All form a ring and travel C-C with the above step, each man falling in behind his own partner so that first woman leads into the circle. All turn R about as described above and repeat the movement C, the men returning to their own line on the last two bars.	17–32

Finish facing forward with arms raised, sounding the castanets on first beat only.

MUIÑEIRA

From Galicia. Noted by Lucile Armstrong
Arranged by Arnold Foster

FIGURE II

a Begin with r foot and sound castanets on each step.

	A
Two walking steps forward, turn R about with feet together and hold position.	1–2
Repeat, travelling to back of dance-space.	3–4
Repeat all, finishing with a turn inward to face partners.	5–8

b Begin with foot nearest front and sound castanets—slow, slow, quick, quick, slow.

(Man's step:) Hop on r foot, pointing l foot to side.	9
Hop on r foot, placing l foot to toe of r foot. 3 stamps—l r l—keeping l foot in front (1 & 2).	10
Repeat with hop on l foot.	11–12
(Women begin on l foot, using same step.) Repeat all, finishing with feet together and facing each other.	13–16

CHORUS

	B
As described above. Finish facing each other.	17–32

FIGURE III: Media Luna. See Plate 4.

	A
Man begins on l foot, woman on r foot, shoulders always swaying over advancing foot. Man's step only described:	
Skip forward on l foot, raising r leg backward with knee bent, r foot under l knee; skip backward on r foot, raising l leg forward with knee bent, l foot in front of r knee.	1
Skip on l foot, placing it behind r foot; skip sideways on r foot; skip on l foot, placing it in front of r foot.	2

Plate 3
Andalusia: Panaderos

The pattern described is that of a half-moon, the woman always in front of the man on the first of the 5 steps.

Repeat the sequence, beginning on the second half of bar 3—man on r foot, woman on l foot—and retracing the pattern. || 3–4

Repeat the whole sequence so that the series of 5 steps is danced six times, the man always on the outside of the woman and partners looking at one another on first skip. || 5–15

Finish with feet together on 1st beat of bar 16, and hold position. || 16

CHORUS || B
As before, to finish facing forward. || 17–32

FIGURE IV || A
Sound castanets: slow, slow, quick, quick, slow.

All spring r foot in front of l foot, leaving l leg straight behind (coupé over); slow. Spring l foot behind r foot, leaving r leg straight in front (coupé under); slow. || 1

3 stamps r l r, keeping r foot in front—quick, quick, slow. || 2

Repeat all, beginning with l foot and turning R to face back of dance-space on the 3 stamps. || 3–4

Repeat coupés, beginning on r and l feet, turning R to face forward on last 3 stamps. || 5–8

Repeat the whole figure, finishing with feet together to face partner, omitting the last 3 stamps. || 9–16

CHORUS || B
As described, to finish facing partner. || 17–32

FIGURE V: Media Luna turning. As in Figure III, but dancers make a complete turn outward on third, fourth and fifth skip of each series.	A 1–16
CHORUS As described, except that the second half is used as an exit—the first man (in the set dance) leading the other dancers in any undulating pattern he desires. The B music may be repeated until the dancers are off the dancing-place.	B As often as desired

PLAYING OF CASTANETS

Simple method. String of castanets on middle finger. Both hands sound the 1st and 4th beats of each bar—except bars 8, 16, 24, 32, when only the 1st beat is sounded.

Correct method. String of castanets either side of middle joint of both thumbs. Right hand: an even roll from fifth to first fingers preceding each 1st and 4th beat. These are marked by the left hand, as in simple method.

The 1st beat only of every eighth bar is sounded by both castanets simultaneously.

In Muiñeira Fig. II*b* and Fig. IV the rhythm of slow, slow, quick, quick, slow should be played.

For castanet accompaniment of Seguidillas Sevillanas see also page 32.

MOVEMENTS AND STEPS
IN SEGUIDILLAS SEVILLANAS

The arm movements are continuous on the whole. The arms are never quite straight, and when held above the head they are held as far back as possible—not slightly forward as in the other dances. One arm is always above the head. Each arm takes 6 beats to go once out to side, down, round and up to place above head. Arms work alternately.

The back is very arched, especially in all the movements when partners change places with one another. During these crossing movements both dancers look towards one another and lean sideways and backwards.

The legs are never quite straightened, even when the foot is raised as high as possible.

The head generally turns over the free shoulder (the side of the lower arm), and partners look at one another during most of the movements. Quick tossing movements of the head are characteristic, especially when the leg is being kicked forward or sideways, and at the finish. The general poise of the chin gives an arrogant appearance.

The castanets are used as in Muiñeira—see 'correct method', page 31—but the rhythm is different. The easiest rhythm is called 'Aria, Aria, Pita'—a mnemonic formula, thus:

Ari-á, Ari-á, Pi-tá
and 1 and 2 and 3

i.e. three beats (one bar) for the whole rhythm. On each 'Ari-á' roll four fingers of the right hand beginning with the little finger, left hand beating the á of 'Ari-á', making five sounds in all. On 'Pi-tá' the right hand sounds Pi, the left hand sounds tá, two sounds in all.

STEPS

PART I: *Paso de Entrada.* This step is done on the spot, shoulders, hips and legs in Open Line, i.e. l side over l foot; r shoulder, arm and leg over r foot, etc. Start with feet in 3rd position, l foot forward, angle of 45°. ‖ MUSIC

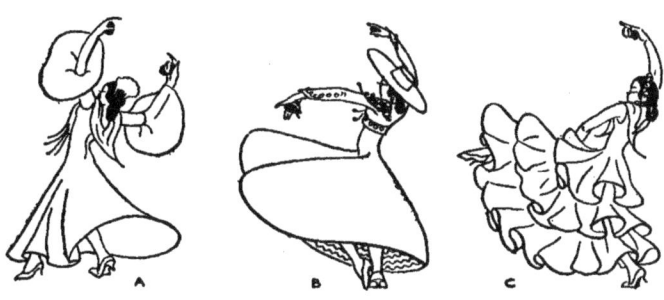

1 Step diagonally forward on l foot. Body bends to R, l hip leading. (See sketch A.) Partners face one another diagonally. Click castanets once in each hand.	Bar *1* Beats: 1
2 Close r foot behind l foot (5th position). Body nearly upright. Beat castanets against one another above head (N.B., this only happens the first time, not on any repeat of the step).	2
3 Step diagonally back on r foot. Body begins to bend to L. Click castanets once in each hand, as Beat 1.	3
4 Place l toe to r toe (5th position). Body bends slightly to L. (See sketch B.)	Bar *2* Beats: 1
5 Kick l leg forward outward—foot high but knee slightly bent. Body upright, r arm well up, l arm swings across body to contrast movement with l leg. (See sketch C.)	2
6 Step l foot behind r foot. Body upright, l arm moves round to above the head, r arm still in place above head. Partners have now passed sideways square to one another and are now very slightly to the R.	3

Cambio. (This movement comes at the end of many steps.)	*Bar 1*
1 Place l toe to r toe (5th position). Body bent slightly to R.	Beats: 1
2 Raise l knee to waist level and circle the leg twice from the knee (double rond-de-	2 and
3 jambe) to flick the skirt outwards.	3
4 Stamp l foot beside r foot. Body turns to L so that partners have got r shoulders towards one another. Arms above head and backwards.	*Bar 2* Beats: 1
5 Stamp r foot in front of l foot. Body begins to turn to R.	2
6 Kick l foot forward upward to waist level. Body turns and bends to R so that partners are beginning to face one another. Click castanets together above the head.	3
7 Long step sideways on l foot (lunge step). Body arched back and bent sideways to R; l arm up, r arm moves out to side and down.	*Bar 3* Beats: 1
8, Three steps forward r l r, changing places 9, with partner, passing each other on the 10 L, but facing one another and finishing by curving inward to R to face partner on the wrong side. This step is followed by Paso de Entrada, beginning on 2nd beat of Bar 4 as described in dance notations (page 38); r arm swings round and up above head.	2 & 3 and *Bar 4* Beat 1
PART II	*Bar 1*
1, Place r toe to l toe (5th position) bending 2 both knees slowly for the two counts. Body bends slightly to R. Look over r shoulder, l arm up, r arm shoulder level.	Beats: 1 2
3 Kick r leg sideways to R, knee slightly bent waist-high. (See sketch D.)	3

	Bar 2
4. Step r foot behind l foot.	Beats: 1
5. Step sideways on l foot.	2
6. Step r foot in front of l foot.	3
Repeat, beginning with l foot.	

PART III

The arm movements are similar to some of those in the Cambio, although the steps are slightly different. Part III is therefore described in the Dance notation, page 38.

THE FINISH. (See also Dance notation, page 38.) — Final Chord

The dancers finish with a turn (at the end of Part III) so that l shoulders are towards partners, looking at one another, chins raised so that an arrogant pose is held. (See sketch E. An alternative pose for the finish is shown on Plate 1.) Castanets are clicked separately on final chord.

Note.—Three stages of study are recommended: (1) Every movement should be studied separately in front of a mirror before attempting to put the dance together. Study the illustrations minutely before trying to copy a pose. (2) Practise the castanets without, then with, the music. (3) Practise dance and castanets together.

D

E

SEGUIDILLAS SEVILLANAS

Region   Andalusia.

Character   Quick and gay. The sudden movements of legs and head form a contrast with the supple, continuous movement of body and arms.

Formation   Couple dance, though sometimes done by two women. The dance takes up little dance-space and consists mainly of the crossing and re-crossing of partners.

Dance	MUSIC
Each Figure, called in Spanish a Copla, consists of three parts. Only one Copla with its three parts is described here.	Bars
INTRODUCTION TO COPLA Partners stand side by side in 3rd position (1 foot in front), man on L. Each dancer has 1 hand on hip, r hand to side, and both look at each other. On the last bar the man takes 3 steps (l, r, together) in a semi-circle to face partner—about one yard apart. These 3 steps lead into the first Part.	Intro- duction
PART I: *Paso de Entrada* Both dancers begin on l foot and dance the step, as described above, 4 times, i.e. on l, r, l, r feet.	1–8
Repeat the first 3 beats on l foot, i.e. forward l, close r toe, back r foot.	9
Cambio Dance this once through so that partners have changed places.	10–12

SEGUIDILLAS SEVILLANAS

Noted by Lucile Armstrong
Arranged by Arnold Foster

Play Introduction, then bars 1–12 three times

Paso de Entrada (2nd time)
    Dance all 6 steps of this Paso counting 2,   1–2
3, 1, 2, 3, 1.
Then step sideways on r foot (beat 2); step   3
on l in front of r foot (beat 3). This is
merely a linking step.

PART II (begins on Bar 4)
    Both begin with r foot and dance the step as   4–9
described 3 times, i.e. with r, l, r feet.

Cambio
    As in Part I, dancers returning on own   10–12
track (keeping to R) to finish curving into
own places, to face partners as at beginning.

Paso de Entrada (3rd time)
    Dance all steps beginning on l foot as in   1–2
Part I: 2 3 1, 2 3 1. Step sideways on r
foot but leave l foot free to start next Part.   3
    (beat 2)

PART III (begins on 3rd beat of Bar 3)   3
    Kick l foot forward upward from toe of r   4–5
foot (beat 3); body turns to R as in step
6 of Cambio.
5 walking steps to change places with partner—body and arms as in Cambio 7, 8, 9,
10, but kick r foot upwards as the last   5
step on l foot is placed on ground.   (beat 3)
Repeat the 5 walking steps beginning with   6–7
r foot, returning to places by the same
track. Repeat the crossing and re-crossing   8–11
beginning with l and r feet.

FINISH
    The final held position only is explained in   11
step description. Begin on last beat, l foot   (beat 3)

Plate 4
Galicia: Muiñeira

in 1st position with no change of weight. Castanets click together. Stamp l foot behind r foot, changing weight. Bring r arm down sharply in front of r leg.

12
(beat 1)

Kick r leg forward and circle it in front of l foot, putting some weight on it—the body and feet have now turned to L, r arm circles up and l comes down. Continue turning to L on balls of both feet (assemblé turn) to finish with l shoulders to partner as shown in sketch E.

(beat 2)

(beat 3)
Final
Chord

Head is jerked backwards. As this last movement only takes 4 beats in all, it should be done as quickly as possible (not to strict beats), and the 'Finish' reached and held as long as possible. Castanets click on final chord.

BIBLIOGRAPHY

ALFORD, VIOLET.—'Cantabrian Calendar Customs and Music.' *The Musical Quarterly* (New York), Oct. 1934.

ALFORD, VIOLET, and GALLOP, RODNEY.—*The Traditional Dance*. Methuen, London, 1935.

BOSCH-GIMPERA.—*Etnologia de la Peninsula Iberica*. Barcelona, 1932.

CANCIO, JESÚS.—*Del Solar y de la Raza*. Vol. 2: *Pasajes*. 1928–31.

CARRERAS Y CANDI.—*Folklore y Costumbres de España*. Vol. 2, Barcelona, 1931.

DIXON, PIERSON.—*The Iberians of Spain*. Oxford University Press, 1940.

ELLIS, HAVELOCK.—*The Soul of Spain*. (Chapter on Dancing.) Constable, London, 1908.

FUERTES, SORIANO.—*Historia de la Musica Española*. Madrid.

LAVIGNAC.—*La Musique et la Danse en Espagne*. In: *Encyclopédie de la Musique*, Paris, 1920.

www.ingramcontent.com/pod-product-compliance
Lightning Source LLC
Chambersburg PA
CBHW061743290426
43661CB00127B/971